Guinea Pig Education
2 Cobs Way
New Haw, Addlestone
Surrey
KT15 3AF
Tel: 01932 336553
Website: www.guineapigeducation.co.uk

© Copyright 2013

NO part of this publication may be reproduced, stored or copied for commercial purposes and profit without the prior written permission of the publishers.

ISBN: 978-1-907733-20-8

Written by: Adele Seviour
Edited by: Sally and Amanda Jones
Graphic Design and Illustrations by: Annalisa Jones

For

Rebecca, Joshua, Michelle, Kristina, Nicole, Fleur, Tyler and Harlyn

The tabby cat, with his pattern of dark markings, spots or stripes on a paler background, is the oldest known domestic cat - known to the Romans as felis catus. This time his magic whiskers whisk him away to a Roman town.

Horace lay in the sun on the garden wall. His tabby coat rippled like little grey and white waves on a pond. His whiskers began to twitch. They twitched a bit more. Was he ready for take off? He activated his i-collar. Horace was a magic cat. He was a time traveller.

The noise of a cart, rumbling down the street, woke Horace up and he opened his big, round eyes. Where was he? He was in a busy place. All around him people were chattering. As he padded down the path, he felt the swish of togas and heard the flip flop sound of sandals close to him. He joined the people who were walking. But where were they going? They were walking towards the forum and the cries of traders selling their goods.

> a toga – a white robe worn over a tunic
>
> a forum – a market square

Horace looked all around him curiously. This must be market day he observed. It must be Saturday. He saw that the market square was full of stalls. Each one had a canvas awning to protect the produce from the burning sun.

Now he looked about the square. It had huge columns, but the lower levels of the brick houses were workrooms... or were they shops? They had counters at the front. There were goods displayed on hooks and poles so you could see what was for sale.

i-collar fact

column - a round pillar

awning - a covering to shelter from the sun

A slave bent down to stroke Horace. In his hand was a shopping list. It said he needed to buy:

- BREAD (PANIS)
- VEGETABLES (HOLERIS)
- MEAT (CARO)

Horace followed him to the baker's stall. There were a huge variety of delicious breads; a bread mixed with cream cheese (athletoe); a wheat bread (emmer) and biscuits that soldiers ate, called (buccellatum).

The slave bought some bread made from emmer wheat, for his master, but then he said,
"Please can I also have some bread made with course bran and a little flour for me and my other slaves, (autopyron)."

Horace concluded that slaves did the everyday shopping.

The smell of delicious food made Horace feel hungry. Mouthwatering aromas wafted towards his nose. He thought he might get a take away, but surely they didn't have take aways in Roman times. Horace soon found out that they did. In fact the take away food shop (thermopolia) was doing a roaring trade.

Horace observed that the blocks of flats, called (insula) had no kitchens to cook food. The people were bringing jugs to fill up with spiced wine and pots to fill with stews, beans, lentils, bread and even porridge. The taverns sold hot, cheap food all day.

But what was that familiar smell? He could smell his favourite food from home. Horace followed the scent and it led him to the fish stall. Yum, yum! What was on the menu today? It was oysters, all the way from Colchester. They have come a long way Horace's i-collar explained. Packed in iced water, they travelled to Rome on the back of mules from Colchester. Horace mewed loudly because he wanted one. The fishmonger saw Horace and threw him a morsel of fish to try. Yuk! It was dried and salted. It was so disgusting he spat it out.

i-collar fact

<u>oyster</u> – a shellfish

<u>Garum sauce</u> – was made from fermented fish and sold in little pots. This fish sauce had a powerful flavour that probably helped to disguise the taste of fish or meat that was often not fresh.

Horace followed another scent. It led him to the butcher's shop, where there were joints of meat hanging from a rail. A slave was waiting for his order, as the butcher weighed it out on the scales.

There was a huge variety of meat: pigeons, doves, thrushes and partridges. There were also mice, lamb, goat, wild boar, hares, venison and suckling pig. He mewed loudly to ask the butcher for some food, but a feather ticked Horace's nose and he let out a huge sneeze.

"shoo", said the butcher.

Horace saw some rich people in front of him. He knew they were rich because the man was wearing a white toga and his wife was wearing a deep blue stolla. He also knew they were rich because rich people only went shopping to buy expensive goods or new slaves. These people were in a furniture shop. They were looking for a new wooden bed and it was highly decorated in gold and turquoise patterns. There was a wicker chair in the shop with a high back, called a (cathedra), and an ornate table with a marble top.

A craftsman was busy working in the shop. He was making a strong box. It had many keys to lock things up. Was this the answer to Roman security, a system to stop thieves stealing?

All of a sudden, Horrace felt a bit drowsy. He jumped up onto a stall (a scamnum) and curled up tightly for a nap... but he was soon woken up.

"Four thousand denarius," shouted someone loudly. Horace opened one eye. He arched his back, stretched out his two front paws and jumped lightly down. He would investigate. A man was standing on a raised platform in the middle of the market square. A slave man was for sale. Horace couldn't believe his eyes. There were two rich Romans bidding to buy him, because they wanted him as a teacher for their children. The auctioneer was pushing the price up and up.

"See how healthy he is," he said, "look what good white teeth he has got," he added, "and there's a bonus... he even speaks Greek," he continued. Horace concluded that he must be telling the truth or he would get into trouble with the market inspector. "Seven thousand, eight thousand... SOLD, to the man on the right. Sold to Dionysius."

To Horace's horror yet more men stepped onto the platform. These men were prisoners of war, who had been kidnapped by Roman pirates. Now the trader continued,

"We have here a fine body of men suitable for hard work," he called. Horace could see the fear on their faces, as they contemplated whether they would go to a good or bad home. The auction began.

"One thousand denarius..." shouted one.

"One thousand, five hundred..." shrieked another.

"Sold to the man on the left."

```
i-collar fact
money – 16 donkeys were worth one denarius.
```

Horace wondered over to the next stall, when bang, wallop, something hit him full on the head,

"Ouch!" he mewed as the apple rolled away, but where had it come from? Horace stood back and gaped at the beautiful stall in front of him. It was so colourful. Horace played a guessing game and wondered how many fruits and vegetables were on sale here.

There were: purple figs, black grapes, green olives, sticks of celery, lettuces and cabbages, shallots, asparagus tips, red and green apples, golden onions, red radishes, rosy red plums and cherries, turnips, wild blackberries, ripe raspberries, juicy strawberries, purple damsons, blue mulberries and sweet chestnuts.

He thought, "Wow! Like the humans eat at home."

Now Horace's ears pricked up. Amongst the hustle and bustle and the chitter chatter of the crowds he could hear something. It was a tap, tap, tap! He followed the sound to a workshop, where an apprentice was repairing a pair of sandals called (caligae) Horace saw that they were military sandals, and they were strong. They had patterns of iron nails, designed for soldiers to wear who would do miles of marching.

A slave was helping her mistress to choose an elegant pair of sandals, but there was too much choice, as there were so many boots and sandals hanging up outside.

What was that? Something glinting in the sun caught Horace's eye and he went over to investigate. It was the silver smith's stall. He was making a beautiful hand mirror in his work shop. He had a jewellery store selling gold necklaces set with precious stones; earrings in the shapes of dolphins and ducks; dangling strings set with rubies and sapphires and silver rings set with amber stones and in the shape of snakes. There were also brooches and hairpins. This dazzling array of glitzy jewels made his head spin.

Horace paused to recover and then he listened to some street musicians who were playing a tune to earn a few coins from the shoppers. There was a young man playing an instrument called the tibiae and another shook the sistrum. Horace thought, "This is very good," and he did a little cat dance.

A tibiae – is a set of double pipes
Sistrum – is a musical instrument shaped like a rattle

Next, Horace wandered from shop to shop listening to the street traders selling their wares:

- "Come and buy... some finely woven wools – linens and silks from China and cotton from India."

- "Have your togas dry cleaned here... Our men (called fullers) can bleach your togas on frames over pots of burning sulphur. They will put them on a mixture of water and clay and tread on them to get the dirt out. When they are dry, they will be folded flat on a press. We guarantee they will come out sparkling white."

- "Wealthy Roman men and women, come to our perfumery and buy our expensive perfumes, presented in little glass onyx jars. Ladies, we have make up made from lead to make your powdered faces beautiful. We have charcoal to darken your eyes. We have a revolutionary new product made from dregs of red wine and red ochre that you can wear as lipstick. Also check out our beautiful gold, jewelled pins and combs for your hair. Don't forget it is recommended now that you use toothpaste. It is sold in little pots, so you better off people had better use it. You men, baldness is no longer a deformity because we have some good wigs. Our best blond wigs even come from German slave girls."

- "Come to the chemist shop to buy your special herbs and potions…" The pungent smell of herbs reached Horace's nose, as the chemist ground them up in front of him. But what were all these other powders for?

Horace switched on his i-collar to search the web for more information:

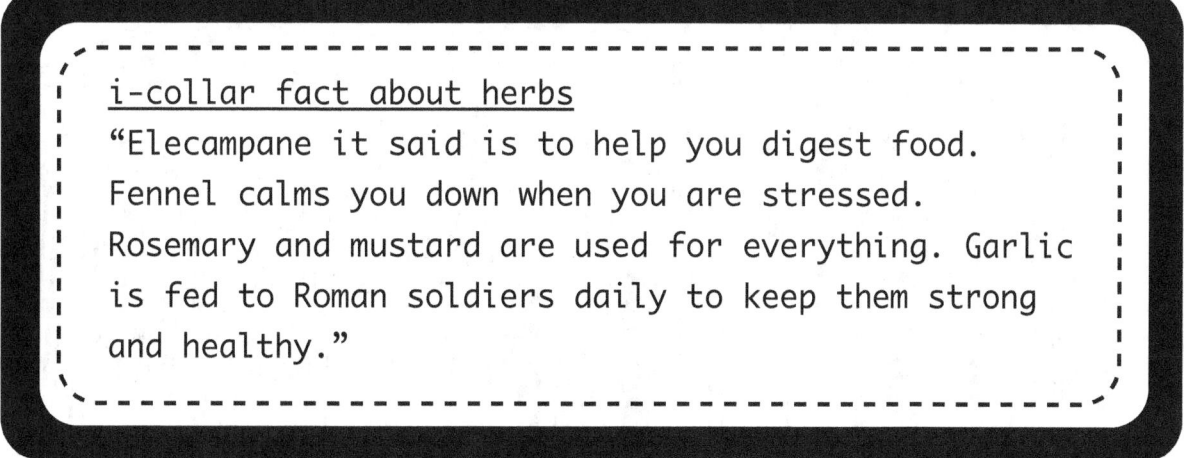

i-collar fact about herbs
"Elecampane it said is to help you digest food. Fennel calms you down when you are stressed. Rosemary and mustard are used for everything. Garlic is fed to Roman soldiers daily to keep them strong and healthy."

His i-collar also told him some surprising facts.

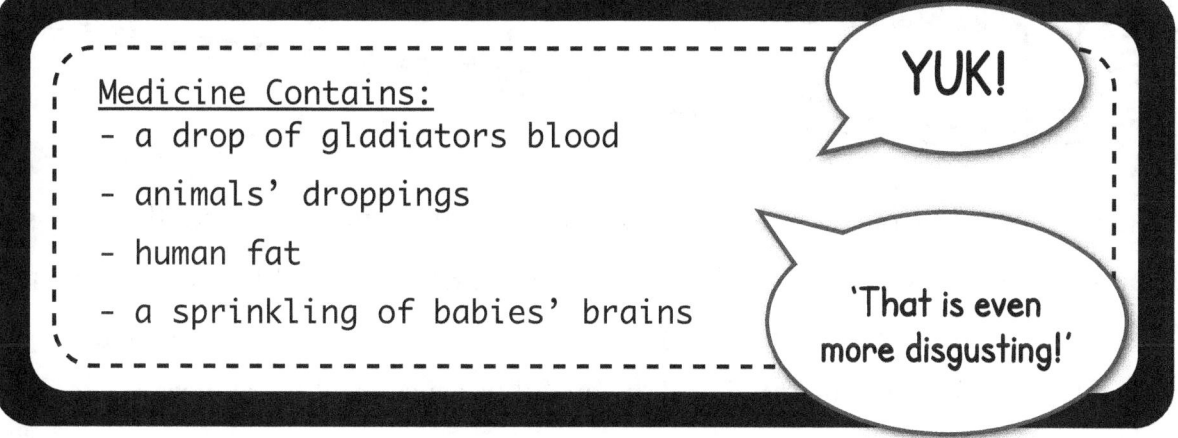

Medicine Contains:
- a drop of gladiators blood
- animals' droppings
- human fat
- a sprinkling of babies' brains

YUK!

'That is even more disgusting!'

Then his i-collar said,

"If you have a baby who is teething, the Romans advise you to rub the blood of a hare on his gums."
But if you don't fancy any of these – why not buy a cygnet ring with a picture of the god Hygeia, who will help you ward off all illness.

Enough for one day of the market square, thought Horace.

At last Horace reached the corner of the square and he padded on his little paws into the next street.

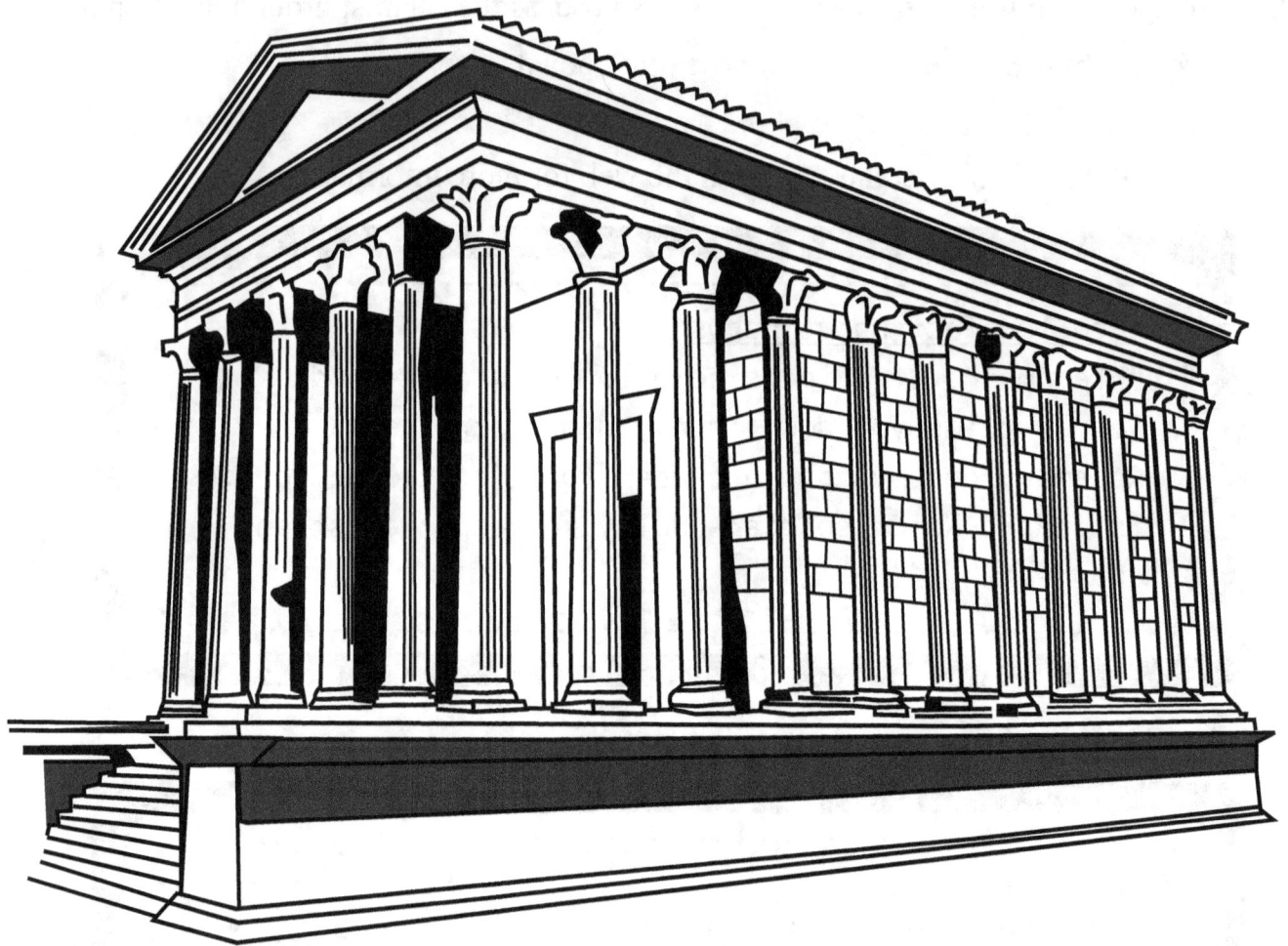

Horace blinked. In front of him was a huge temple. It shone magnificently because the building was covered in a thin layer of marble. Horace was filled with curiosity. He had to go in and have a look. He stepped inside. No one seemed to take any notice of him. Wow! It was filled with beautiful treasures and there were lots of priests and priestesses looking after them. They glared down at Horace. Cats were not welcome in temples.

Horace paused. He must ask his i-collar...

> "In ancient Rome, there were many temples dedicated to gods and goddesses. People feared them and sought their favour."

Who were all these gods? Horace typed into his i-collar.

JUPITER	god of light	KING OF GODS
JUNO	goddess of women & children	QUEEN OF GODS
VESTA	goddess of the hearth	
MARS	god of war	
SATURNUS	god of agriculture	
CERES	goddess of crops	
MINERVA	goddess of wisdom, healing, arts and crafts	
VENUS	goddess of love	
DIANA	goddess of the moon	
NEPTUNUS	god of the waters	
VULCAN	god of fire	
APOLLO	god of music	
MERCURY	god of commerce and trade	
PLUTO	god of the underworld	

Horace padded back outside into the sunlight. He noticed that there were some people making offerings at an alter outside the temple. "That's because, they are ordinary people and not allowed inside the temple," thought Horace. These people had brought model ears and legs with them as part of their offering so that the gods would know which part of the person's body needed help.

It was at this point, that Horace heard cheering. He followed the sound until he came to a circular building with seats all the way round it. It was an ampitheatre and it was used for games and shows. It had been built by the Emperor or rich Romans so they would win the favour of the public, because they let the public go in free. Horace read the programme on the walls. It said:

ALL DAY ENTERTAINMENT

WARM UP ACTS

- SEE TWO <u>WILD ELEPHANTS</u> FIGHT FOR THEIR LIVES. OGLE AT OUR AMAZING ACROBATS AND CLIMBERS. SEE WILD ANIMALS FROM FOREIGN LANDS – BEARS, TIGERS, WOLVES AND HYENAS WILL BE RELEASED AND BANDS OF ARCHERS WILL SEE HOW MANY THEY CAN HIT.

- <u>LIVE ENTERTAINMENT</u> ON THE MAIN STAGE

- SEE <u>BRUTAL FIGHTS</u> BETWEEN GLADIATORS TRAINED IN THE MOST RENOWNED SCHOOLS. SEE IF MARCUS CAN SURVIVE THE FIGHT TO WIN HIS FREEDOM.

Horace watched a lightly armed gladiator (called a thraciam), stab his foe to death with a dagger. Horace did not like this at all and he raced to the nearest exit quickly.

Now the light was fading and night was drawing in. Horace was on a road, but oh no, it was getting really noisy. There were many wheeled vehicles. There were carts and there were chariots and they had all come out on the road at night because they were not allowed to make deliveries during the day. The laws forbid it. Instead they had to make their deliveries at night.

Horace put his paws over his ears. It was so noisy. He began to look for somewhere to rest. He went towards the next largest building. It said 'free to all citizens' on a sign by the door. Horace thought, "It is a bit like a leisure centre. It has hot baths, massage rooms, shops, restaurants, a library and a sports ground." It was the public baths. Horace thought, "I need a bath, after all this travelling," so he went in. He couldn't find any soap and had to use a strange implement, called a strigil, to scrape the oil, the sweat and dirt from his stripy fur with olive oil. He cleaned out his ears with the ear scoop, filed his claws with nail cleaner and he plucked out a few stray hairs from his coat with the tweezers. After this, he went into the hot room, where sweet steam swirled in mists in front of his eyes. He felt so hot, he felt so dizzy that he settled down to go to sleep. But when he opened his eyes he found himself lying back in the hot sun on the garden wall. What a lot he had learned about a Roman town.

i-collar Information Page

Horace's i-collar tells him lots of facts about a Roman town.
LEARN ROMAN TOWN FACTS FROM THE i-COLLAR.

What shops are in a Roman town?

Weavers – sold cloth

Dry Cleaners/Toga cleaners.
Men, called fullers, put the togas in a mixture of water and special clay, trod on them to get the dirt out and then dried them on a frame. The togas were then pressed in a machine.

Chemists
Sold medicines containing gladiators blood, animal droppings, human fat and a sprinkling of baby brains. They sold magic spells, special herbs and potions. The herb, SAGE, was a powerful healer, ROSEMARY was sacred to the Romans, FENNEL was used for its calming properties and ELECAMPANE for digestion. For teething, the Romans recommended a drop of hare's blood be put on the gums.

Jewellers
The jeweller's shop sold signet rings that symbolized health; gold, silver, brass and bronze necklaces, bracelets, brooches and rings set with precious stones. They sold silver hand mirrors and earrings in the shape of dolphins, ducks and snakes and dangly strings of rubies, sapphires and garnets. They sold hairpins and combs carved from bone.

Perfumery
In the perfumery and make up store you could buy make up made of powdered chalk or white lead powder; red ochre blusher and lip colour and charcoal eye shadows. Perfumes were sold in small onyx jars and toothpaste in little jars. At this store rich Romans could purchase wigs.

Furniture shop
Here you could buy plain beds made from wood; as well as some very grand beds, carved in gold with decorated head boards; high backed chairs called cathedra; tables with marble tops and strong boxes and (scamnums) or stools.

i-collar Information Page

Where can I buy food in the Roman town?

Bakers Shop:
The bakers sold (panis) or bread, (athletoe) a bread mixed with cream cheese, (autopyrm) a bread made of course bran; (emmer) a bread made of wheat and (bucellatum) a special bread like a biscuit, given to soldiers.

Butchers:
The butchers sold (caro) or meat. The Romans ate meat from ducks, peacocks, pigeons, doves, thrushes, partridges, dormice, lambs, goats, wild boar, hares, venison and suckling pig.

Hot food shop:
Sold hot, take away food, including, spiced wine, stews, beans, lentils and porridge.

Green Grocer or vegetable shop:
Sold vegetables and fruit, including, apples, figs, black grapes, green olives, celery, lettuce, cabbages, shallots, asparagus, golden onions, radishes, plums, cherries, turnips, blackberries, raspberries, strawberries, mulberries, sweet chestnuts and damsons.

Roman Clothes Explained

Men wore:

- tunics made of wool or linen
- togas were worn in public
- Burris Britannica cloaks were worn in cold weather
- Many different types of sandal
- Caligoe – a military sandal
- Soldiers boots studded with nails

Women wore:

- Innner tunics of wool
- Wealthy women wore Chinese silk or Indian cotton
- Flowing garments called a stolla
- Silk pallas over their tunics, belted at the waist and dyed red, blue, green and saffron yellow

Easy Reader
Exercises

Week One

Monday: Spelling Patterns

a b c d e f g h i j k l m n o p q r s t u v w x y z

bread	dead	healthy	steady	read
feather	measure	wealthy	head	treasure
ready	thread	weather	leather	

Put the words that sound the same in the correct columns.

bread	treasure	healthy	ready

Now put the words in alphabetical order.

....

Tuesday: Comprehension

1. Read the story 'Horace Visits a Roman Town' and answer the questions in short sentences.

   a. Where did Horace find himself?
   b. What day was it?
   c. How did they keep the sun off the stalls?
   d. Who did the everyday shopping?
   e. What type of wheat was the bread made from?

2. Put the correct words in the sentences.

   a. Bread mixed with cream cheese was called ....
   b. The .... food shop was doing a roaring trade.
   c. There were .... packed in iced water.
   d. A .... tickled Horace's nose.
   e. A wicker chair with a high back was called a ....

WEEK 1: Easy Reader

Wednesday: **Homonyms**

A homonym *sounds the same* but has *different meanings*.

1. Write out the sentences and underline the correct word.

    a. It was a sunny day and the sky was *blue/blew*.
    b. She bought some *flower/flour* to make an apple pie.
    c. The ship docked at the *quay/key*.
    d. The *night/knight* was dressed in full armour.
    e. The *plane/plain* took off at ten o' clock.
    f. The *sea/see* was very rough.
    g. I had to *meat/meet* my friend in the park.
    h. It was my job to *peel/peal* the potatoes.
    i. I wash my *hare/hair* everyday.
    j. The *sail/sale* at the store was to last one week.

2. Put the correct word from the list to the phrases.

peace	beach	stairs	pain
key	pane	quay	beech
piece	stares		

    a. opens a lock ...

    b. suffering ...

    c. a flight of steps ...

    d. a sandy shore ...

    e. a kind of tree ...

WEEK 1: Easy Reader

Thursday: **Adverbs**

Adverbs are words that *describe* how actions are done.

Write these sentences and choose the correct adverb from the list to complete the sentence.

quickly	badly	greedily	freely
finely	slowly	exquisitely	

a. Horace walked s............... down the street.
b. The model was f............... dressed.
c. The bracelet was e............... made.
d. Horace g............... ate the fish.
e. The wooden ornament was b............... carved.
f. Horace left the temple q...................
g. The flag fluttered f............... in the breeze.

Write these sentences and underline the adverbs.

a. Horace crept silently from the room.
b. The fog spread rapidly over the town.
c. Horace slept peacefully on the stool.
d. The gladiator fought bravely.
e. Horace looked hungrily at the fish stall.
f. In the arena the lion roared loudly.

WEEK 1: Easy Reader

Friday: Design a Poster

Design a poster for your shop.

GET YOUR FISH FROM ROBERTUS.

The **BEST** in Rome.

You will find us ....
....
....
....

Look at the variety ....
....
....
....

Healthy eating ....
....
....
....

For Sale

Clothes for the best dressed ....
....
....
....

All Colours ....
....
....
....

The **BEST** furniture in the world.

Beautiful decorated beds ....
....
....
....
....

Easy Reader
Exercises

Week Two

Monday: **Collective Nouns**

Write out the sentences in your book and choose the correct collective noun to compete the sentence.

clutch   gaggle   pack   swarm   crate

1. A .... of birds flew off into the sunset.
2. A .... of fruit was delivered to the vegetable shop.
3. A .... of geese waddled down to the pond.
4. The .... of wolves went hunting.
5. A .... of bees came out of the hive.

Sounds

Read through the story and find the sounds which go with the following phrases.

1. The .... of togas.
2. The .... of sandals.
3. 4000 denaru someone ....
4. Horace left the temple and heard some ....

WEEK 2: Easy Reader

Tuesday: **Compound Words**

A word which is at its *simplest* form is called a <u>primary word</u>.   e.g.   table   house

If we *combine* two primary words we get a <u>compound</u> word.   e.g.   blackboard

---

1. See how many compound words you can make from the list below.

   e.g.   *toothpaste*

tooth	fast	break
paste	lip	light
sun	stick	house
shop	work	hold

2. Now make up your own sentences using the compund words you have found.

3. Using a dictionary see how many compound words you can find. Make a list of them.

WEEK 2: Easy Reader

Wednesday: **Punctuation**

Using capital letters, full stops and speech marks, punctuate the following sentences.

1. horace opened one eye

2. he arched his back stretched out his two front paws and jumped lightly down

3. the auctioneer was pushing the price up see how healthy he is

4. sold to dionysius for 8,000

5. a fine body of men suitable for hard work the trader called

6. toothpaste was sold in little pots but only better off people used it

7. the fishmonger threw Horace a morsel of fish

8. horace could hear tap tap tap

9. the chemists shop sold many potions

10. the games lasted all day

WEEK 2: Easy Reader

Thursday: **Spelling Patterns**

1. Write out the following sentences in your book. Choose the correct word to complete the sentences.

   gnome   gnat   sign

   design   reign   campaign

   b. Please .... on the dotted line.

   c. The .... wore a red feather in his cap.

   d. The soldier's .... was successful.

   e. The King's .... lasted ten years.

   f. The floral .... of roses won first prize.

   g. Her lump was caused by the bite of a ....

2. Put these 'gr' words in alphabetical order.

   grub   grin   grab   groove

   green   grant   greed   grass

   grind   grocer

3. Make five of your own sentences using these words.

WEEK 2: Easy Reader

Friday: **Roman Numerals**

This shows how the Romans counted.

I	1	XI	11	XXI	21
II	2	XII	12	XXII	22
III	3	XIII	13	XXIII	23
IV	4	XIV	14	XXIV	24
V	5	XV	15	XXV	25
VI	6	XVI	16	XXVI	26
VII	7	XVII	17	XXVII	27
VIII	8	XVIII	18	XXVIII	28
IX	9	XIX	19	XXIX	29
X	10	XX	20	XXX	30

What dates are these?
Using the chart above, write the Roman and the English dates.

XIV December   XXV Februarius   II Maius

XIV October   XVII Aprilis   VI Junius

XXII Martius   VIII November   XI Augustus

III Julius   XXIX Januarius   IX September

Draw four pictures: spring, summer, autumn, winter. Put the Roman names underneath. Use plain A4 paper and design an edge round the outside. Look at the Roman patterns.

Higher Level Exercises

Week One

Monday: Spelling Patterns

Put the following words in the correct columns.

bread	feather	head	dead
weather	read	thread	leather
ready	measure	steady	treasure

bread	feather	ready

Now put them in alphabetical order.

Put the following words in the correct columns.

about	shout	cloud	sprout
wound	round	pound	mount
proud			

sound	trout

Write the plurals of the following words.

mountain	cloud	sound	fountain
shout	bound	hair	scout
round	ground		

WEEK 1: Higher Level

Tuesday: **Comprehension**

1. Re-read through the story 'Horace Visits A Roman Town. Answer the following questions.

   a. Where did Horace find himself and where were the people going?

   b. Why was it a busy day?

   c. How did the people know what goods were being sold?

   d. What was the slave shopping for?

   e. What type of bread was given to the soldiers?

   f. Name some of the food that you could buy at the hot food stalls.

   g. What type of food was sold in the butchers shop?

   h. Why did the box have to have a complicated series of locks?

   i. Why was the rich Roman buying a slave?

   j. Name ten items on the vegetable stall.

WEEK 1: Higher Level

Wednesday: **Homonyms**

Homonyms are words that are *pronounced alike* but *differ in meanings*.

1. Make short sentences one for each word, showing the correct use.

blew	blue
flour	flower
hair	hare
key	quay
knight	night
meat	meet
peel	peal
plain	plane
sail	sale
sea	see

2. From these words, write out the phrases with the correct word at the side.

| peace | beach | stairs | pain | key |
| pane | quay | beech | piece | stares |

a. opens lock ....
   harbour ....

b. suffering ....
   piece of glass ....

c. a flight of steps ....
   to look fixedly ....

d. sandy shore ....
   kind of tree ....

e. quietness ....
   a part of something ....

WEEK 1: Higher Level

Thursday: **Adverbs**

Adverbs are words that *describe* how *actions are done*.

e.g.   Horace walked <u>slowly</u> down the street.

> The word slowly tells you how Horace walked. The majority of adverbs are formed from adjectives by adding '**ly**'.

1. Form adverbs from:

   quick   **elegant**   **curl**   **fine**   **light**

   clean   **bad**   **thin**   **special**   **free**

2. Now, use the adverbs in your own sentences.

Comparison of adverbs by adding 'er' and 'est'

	e.g.	quick	quicker	quickest
1.		light	lighter	lightest
2.		fine	......	......
3.		quick	......	......
4.		thin	......	......
5.		clean	......	......

WEEK 1: Higher Level

Friday: **Design a Poster**

Design a poster for your shop.

GET YOUR FISH FROM ROBERTUS.

The <u>BEST</u> in Rome.

You will find us ....
....
....
....

Look at the variety ....
....
....
....

Healthy eating ....
....
....
....

For Sale

Clothes for the best dressed ....
....
....
....

All Colours ....
....
....
....

The <u>BEST</u> furniture in the world.

Beautiful decorated beds ....
....
....
....
....
....

Higher Level Exercises

Week Two

Monday: Collective Nouns

Insert a suitable collective noun in each of the spaces.

| crate | batch | bunch | sheaf | clutch |
| flock | gaggle | pack | swarm | herd |

1. a .... of wolves
2. a .... of birds
3. a .... of flowers
4. a .... of geese
5. a .... of corn
6. a .... of furniture
7. a .... of bread
8. a .... of eggs
9. a .... of bees
10. a .... of elephants

To each line add three words from the list below that belong to the group.

hens	primrose	red	wheat	America	poodle
butter	strawberry	ducks	bluebell	blue	oats
Italy	colic	sugar	apple	geese	daisy
green	barley	Denmark	Beagle	tea	oranges

1. poulty ....
2. flowers ....
3. colours ....
4. cereals ....
5. countries ....
6. dogs ....
7. groceries ....
8. fruit ....

WEEK 2: Higher Level

Tuesday: **Compound Words**

A word in its *simplest* form is called a <u>primary word</u>.

e.g.   table   house

If we *combine* two primary words to form one word we get a <u>compound</u> word.

e.g.   blackboard

---

1. These words are found in the story. Form compound words from the following.

work	paste	smith	tooth
shop	silver	rooms	thunder
way	door	bolt	neck
men	crafts	lace	out
stick	lip	side	break
like	war	fast	work

2. Find these sentences in the story and put in the correct compound word.

   a. *Under the colonnade the lower levels of the houses were shops and ......*

   b. *A .... was working on a strong box.*

   c. *It was a ..... where an apprentice was repairing a pair of military sandals.*

   d. *The .... was making a beautiful hand mirror.*

   e. *....... was sold in little pots.*

3. Now make up three more sentences using compound words from the list.

WEEK 2: Higher Level

Wednesday: **Punctuation**

1. Copy out the following using capital letters, commas, full stops and speech marks.

   4,000 denaru someone shouted Horace opened one eye he arched his back stretched out his two front paws and jumped lightly down he went to investigate a slave was standing on a raised platform he was wanted by two rich romans as a teacher for their children the auctioneer was pushing the price up see how healthy he is good white teeth and he speaks greek he had to tell the truth or he would be in trouble with the market inspector 7,000 8,000 sold to Dionysius for 8,000

 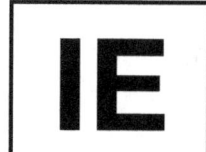

Thursday: **Spelling Patterns**

1. Put these words in alphabetical order.

   knuckle   *knock*   *knit*   *knee*   *knob*
   knife   *knew*   *know*   *knot*   *knight*

2. Put the correct word in the following phrases.

   1. I hurt my ....
   2. The .... would not turn.
   3. ...., fork and spoon.
   4. The .... fell off his horse.
   5. I .... my tables.
   6. He .... me from school.
   7. .... the door loudly.
   8. Tie the .... tightly.
   9. I hurt the ...... on my index finger.
   10. My grandmother said, "I will .... you some gloves."

3. From the following words make your own sentences.

   priest   *pier*   *shield*   *niece*   *piece*
   thief   *chief*   *believe*   *brief*

WEEK 2: Higher Level

Friday: **Comprehension**

Horace followed the sound and came to the ampitheatre. This was a circular building with seats all the way round. The ampitheatre was used for games and shows. They lasted all day, with a break at midday for fresh sand to be spread. The games were paid for by the emperor, and important Romans, to gain popularity. The public went in free. Horace read the notices around the walls, 'See two wild elephants fight to the death. Come see the acrobats and conjurers.' These were the warm up acts before the blood sports. In the mornings, wild animals from foreign lands: bears, elephants, lions, tigers, wolves, hyenas, were released and bands of archers came and shot them. The gladiator fights were quite brutal. There were many different types of gladiators. They were trained in special schools. If they were lucky they survived to win their freedom. Horace watched a lightly armed gladiator called a Thracian carrying a curved dagger and a very small shield, fight a Retiarius or net man. He carried a weighted net to catch his foe and a Neptune Trident to stab him.

Now answer the following questions in sentences.

1. *Describe the Ampitheatre.*

2. *What was the ampitheatre used for?*

3. *Who paid for the games and how much did the public pay to go in?*

4. *What types of animals could you see?*

5. *What were the warm up shows?*

6. *Where were the gladiators trained?*

7. *What weapons did a Thracian carry?*

8. *What did the Retiarius fight with?*

WEEK 2: Higher Level

Friday: **Roman Calendar**

Our calendar is based on the Roman one of 46 BC.

Januarius	Februarius	Martius
Aprilis	Maius	Junius
Julius	Augustus	September
October	November	December

This shows how the Romans counted.

I	1	**XI**	11	**XXI**	21
II	2	**XII**	12	**XXII**	22
III	3	**XIII**	13	**XXIII**	23
IV	4	**XIV**	14	**XXIV**	24
V	5	**XV**	15	**XXV**	25
VI	6	**XVI**	16	**XXVI**	26
VII	7	**XVII**	17	**XXVII**	27
VIII	8	**XVIII**	18	**XXVIII**	28
IX	9	**XIX**	19	**XXIX**	29
X	10	**XX**	20	**XXX**	30

Write down your birthday in Roman words and numbers.

What dates are these? Write the Roman and the English dates.

XIV December	XXV Februarius	II Maius
XIV October	XVII Aprilis	VI Junius
XXII Martius	VIII November	XI Augustus
III Julius	XXIX Januarius	IX September

Draw four pictures: spring, summer, autumn, winter. Put the Roman names underneath. Use plain A4 paper and design an edge round the outside. Look at the Roman patterns.

ANSWERS

EASY READER EXERCISES

MONDAY: Week One

bread	treasure	healthy	ready
read	measure	wealthy	steady
thread	feather		
head	leather		
dead	weather		

....

bread   dead   feather   head   healthy   leather   measure

read   ready   steady   treasure   wealthy   weather

TUESDAY: Week One

1. Horace found himself in a busy place.
2. It was Saturday, market day.
3. Each stall had a canvas cover.
4. Slaves did the everyday shopping.
5. Bread was made from emmer wheat.

....

1. athletoe
2. take away
3. oysters
4. feather
5. cathedra

WEDNESDAY: Week One

1. blue
2. flour
3. quay
4. knight
5. plane
6. sea
7. meet
8. peel
9. hair
10. sale

1. key
2. pain
3. stairs
4. beach
5. beech

ANSWERS

EASY READER EXERCISES

THURSDAY: Week One

1. slowly
2. finely
3. exquisitely
4. greedily
5. badly
6. quickly
7. freely

....

1. silently
2. rapidly
3. peacefully
4. bravely
5. hungrily
6. loudly

MONDAY: Week Two

1. flock
2. crate
3. gaggle
4. pack
5. swarm

....

1. swish
2. flip flop
3. shouted
4. cheering

TUESDAY: Week Two

toothpaste   breakfast   lipstick   sunlight   household   workshop

WEDNESDAY: Week Two

1. Horace opened one eye.
2. He arched his back, stretched out his two front paws and jumped lightly down.
3. The auctioneer was pushing the price up, 'See how healthy he is," he shouted.
4. "Sold to Dionysius for 8,000," he proclaimed.
5. "A fine body of men, suitable for hard work," the trader called.
6. Toothpaste was sold in little pots but only better off people used it.
7. The fishmonger threw Horace a morsel of fish.
8. Horace could hear tap! tap! tap!
9. The chemist's shop sold many potions.
10. The games lasted all day.

ANSWERS

EASY READER EXERCISES

THURSDAY: Week Two

1. sign
2. gnome
3. campaign
4. reign
5. design
6. knot

....

grab grant grass greed green grin grind grocer groove grub

FRIDAY: Week Two

14th December, 25th February, 2nd May, 14th October, 17th April, 6th June, 22nd March, 8th November, 11th August, 3rd July, 29th January, 9th September

ANSWERS

HIGHER READER EXERCISES

MONDAY: Week One

bread	feather	ready
head	weather	steady
dead	leather	
read	measure	
thread	treasure	

Alphabetical Order

bread, dead, feather, head, leather, measure, read, ready, steady, thread, treasure, weather

sound		trout
round	pound	about
cloud	proud	sprout
wound		shout
		mount

Plurals

mountains, clouds, sounds, fountains, shouts, bounds, hours, scouts, rounds, grounds

ANSWERS

HIGHER READER EXERCISES

TUESDAY: Week One

1. Horace found himself in a busy street and the people were going to market.
2. It was a busy day because it was market day.
3. The goods were displayed on hooks or poles to show what was being sold or made.
4. The slave was shopping for panis (bread), holerius (vegetables) and cubis (meat).
5. The soldiers had buccellatum a bread like a biscuit.
6. At the hot food stalls you could buy porridge, stews, beans, lentils, bread, wine and more.
7. In the butchers shop you could buy pigeons, doves, lambs, goats, wild boar, hares, venison, ducks, peacocks.
8. The box had a series of locks to stop it be in burgled.
9. They wanted the slave to teach their children
10. The vegetable stall sold – grapes, lettuce, cabbages, apples, turnips, strawberries etc.

WEDNESDAY: Week One

a. opens lock — key
   harbour — quay

b. suffering — pain
   piece of glass — pane

c. a flight of steps — stairs
   to look fixedly — stares

d. sandy shore — beach
   kind of tree — beech

e. quietness — peace
   a part of something — piece

THURSDAY: Week One

quickly   elegantly   curly   finely   lightly

cleanly   badly   thinly   specially   freely

....

1. light, lighter, lightest
2. fine, finer, finest
3. quick, quicker, quickest
4. thin, thinner, thinnest
5. clean, cleaner, cleanest

....

MONDAY: Week Two

1. pack
2. flock
3. bunch
4. gaggle
5. sheaf
6. crate
7. batch
8. clutch
9. swarm
10. herd

1. poultry – hens, ducks, geese
2. flowers – primrose, bluebell, daisy
3. colours – red, blue, green
4. cereals – wheat, oats, barley
5. countries – America, Italy, Denmark
6. Dogs – Poodle, Collie, Beagle
7. Groceries – butter, sugar, tea
8. Fruits – strawberry, apple, oranges

ANSWERS

HIGHER READER EXERCISES

TUESDAY: Week Two

work/shop, work/rooms, tooth/paste, silver/smith, thunder/bolt, door/way, neck/lace, crafts/men, out/side, lip/stick, break/fast, war/like

....

a. workrooms
b. craftsman
c. workshop
d. silversmith
e. toothpaste

WEDNESDAY: Week Two

"4,000 denaru," someone shouted. Horace opened one eye. He arched his back, stretched out his two front paws and jumped lightly down. He went to investigate. A slave was standing on a raised platform. He was wanted by two rich Romans as a teacher for their children. The auctioneer was pushing the price up. "See how healthy he is, good white teeth and he speaks Greek." He had to tell the truth or he would be in trouble with the market inspector,
"7,000..."
"8,000," Sold to Dionysius for 8,000."

THURSDAY: Week Two

| knee | knew | knife | knight | knit |
| knob | knock | knot | know | knuckle |

....

1. knee 2. knob 3. knife 4. knight 5. knew 6. knew 7. knock 8. knot
9. knit 10. knuckle

FRIDAY: Week Two

1. The ampitheatre was a circular building with seats all the way round.
2. The ampitheatre was used for games and shows.
3. The emperor and important romans paid for the shows, the public went in free.
4. You would see bears, elephants, lions, tigers, wolves and hyenas.
5. The warm up shows were the acrobats and conjurers.
6. The gladiators were trained in special schools.
7. The Thracian gladiator carried a curved dagger and a small shield.
8. The Retiarii carried a net and a trident.

....

14th December, 25th February, 2nd May, 14th October, 17th April, 6th June, 22nd March, 8th November, 11th August, 3rd July, 29th January, 9th September

www.ingramcontent.com/pod-product-compliance
Lightning Source LLC
Chambersburg PA
CBHW050716090526
44587CB00019B/3399